In the Kitchen with Debby

Favorite Family Recipes

DEBBY GASS

Bless you!
Debby

IN THE KITCHEN WITH DEBBY: Favorite Family Recipes
by Debby Gass
Library of Congress Catalog Card Number: Pending
International Standard Book Number: 1-931727-95
Copyright 2002 by Celebration Enterprises
P.O. Box 1045
Roswell, GA 30077-1045
USA

Cover photographs and photographs on title page and pages 6–7
© Mary Robinette

Synergy Publishers
Gainesville, Florida
USA

Dedication

This book is dedicated to my mum – Helen!
Without you, it would not have been written.
My love of entertaining and cooking comes from you.
To me you are the world's most gracious hostess.

Now that I am grown, I realize the incredible job
you did! Somehow you managed to raise two
children, work full-time, and still have
home-cooked meals on the table every night.

You never missed a birthday or a holiday and I still
remember the smell of my favorite goodies baking in
the oven every weekend. Thank you, I love you!

To all the incredible mums out there – who
"do it all," this book's for you too!

My sister-in-law Ruth Halliday and I
have fun making breakfast!

Contents

"Cheerfully share your home with those who need
a meal or a place to stay for the night.
God has given each of you some special abilities.
Be sure to use them to help each other, passing on to others
God's many kinds of blessings."

2 Peter 4:9–10 TLB

Mum's Home Cookin'

Pork with Apricots

1 pound pork tenderloin, cut into 1-inch pieces
1 onion, finely chopped
1 medium tin apricots, drained, quartered, and juice reserved
1 chicken stock cube, dissolved in $\frac{1}{2}$ cup water
2 tablespoons vinegar
2 tablespoons Worcestershire sauce
1 tablespoon softened brown sugar
1 ounce flour, seasoned with salt and pepper
2 ounces butter

Melt butter in pan, add onion and cook until tender. Toss pork pieces in seasoned flour; add to pan and cook until evenly browned. Remove pork and onion from pan and make a roux with remaining flour and fat. Add chicken stock, vinegar, Worcestershire sauce, sugar, and reserved apricot juice.

Simmer on low heat for 25 minutes. Just before serving, add quartered apricots. Heat gently and serve over rice.

Beef Stroganoff

1 pound fillet or sirloin steak, cut into strips, 2 inches long and ¼ inch thick
2 medium sized onions, finely chopped
4 ounces butter
1 green pepper, cut into strips, seeds discarded
8 ounces button mushrooms, wiped clean and thinly sliced
1 tablespoon Worcestershire sauce
½ cup sour cream (or heavy cream mixed with 1 teaspoon lemon juice)
Salt and pepper to taste
A few sprigs of fresh parsley, finely chopped

Melt half of butter in pan, add onions and cook until golden brown. Add green pepper and mushrooms and cook for 5 minutes until tender. (May add more butter if needed). Remove onions, mushrooms, and peppers from pan – set aside.

Melt remaining butter, add steak and cook for about 4 minutes. Return onion mixture to pan and season with salt and pepper. Stir in sour cream and Worcestershire sauce and blend well. Reheat on low until mixture is hot but not boiling.

Serve over rice and garnish with fresh parsley.

Savory Mince Pancakes

BATTER

4 ounces all purpose flour
1 egg
½ pint (1¼ cups) milk and water, mixed
Pinch of salt

Sift flour and salt into bowl, make a well in the center and add egg. Gradually add the milk and water mixture and beat until it becomes a smooth batter.

Lightly grease frying pan with oil. Heat pan on medium/low setting. Pour in sufficient batter to lightly cover base of pan (pancakes should be thin). Cook 1 minute and flip, then cook 30 seconds or until just set. (Makes 8 pancakes.)

Pancakes can be made ahead, separated with grease-proof paper rounds and stored in the refrigerator.

FILLING

½ pound ground beef
1 medium onion, finely chopped
2 tomatoes, skinned and roughly chopped
1 beef stock cube, dissolved in ½ pint
  (1¼ cups) water

1 tablespoon ketchup
4 tablespoons flour
1 tablespoon olive oil
Pinch of mixed dried herbs
Salt and pepper to taste

Heat oil. Add meat and onions to pan and cook until meat is browned and onion is tender. Stir in flour, dissolved beef stock cube, tomatoes, ketchup, herbs, salt and pepper. Bring mixture to boil, reduce heat and simmer for 40 minutes.

Gently reheat pancakes in oven at 250°. Place warmed pancake on plate, spoon meat mixture in center and fold pancake over meat mixture.

Fudge Fingers

BASE

4 ounces margarine
2 ounces sugar
6 ounces all purpose flour
1 ounce coconut

Mix all ingredients together in a bowl, spread evenly in Swiss roll tin and bake at 350° for 15 minutes until lightly browned. Cool.

TOPPING

1 small tin Nestlé condensed milk
4 ounces margarine
4 ounces sugar
1 dessert spoon of syrup
6 ounces semi-sweet milk chocolate

Melt margarine in saucepan; add milk, sugar, and syrup. Stir over low heat until mixture thickens and becomes a light caramel color. Pour over base and allow to cool.

Melt chocolate in double boiler; pour over fudge and chill in fridge. Cut fudge into finger-sized pieces.

Picnic Slices

4 ounces sugar
4 ounces margarine
4 ounces coconut
2 ounces sultanas (or raisins)
2 ounces red cherries, finely chopped
1 egg, lightly beaten
6 ounces semi-sweet chocolate

Gently melt chocolate in double boiler and pour into Swiss roll tin and chill to set.

Cream margarine; add sugar and egg and mix thoroughly. Add coconut, sultanas and cherries. Spread mixture over set chocolate. Bake at 350° for 15 minutes until golden brown.

My mum, Helen, likes to sample the goodies from the bowl.

Belfast Boiled Cake

1 cup sugar
1 cup cold water
2 cups mixed fruit (raisins, sultanas, currants)
1 cup plain (all-purpose) flour
1 cup self rising flour
4 ounces margarine
1 teaspoon cinnamon
1 teaspoon mixed spice
1 teaspoon baking soda
1 egg

Put sugar, water, fruit, margarine, cinnamon, and mixed spices into saucepan and bring to a boil. Allow to boil rapidly for 2–3 minutes. Remove from heat and allow to cool. Add sifted flour, egg, and baking soda and mix thoroughly. Place in loaf tin and bake at 400° for 1 hour.

*Mum and I have
a little fun with flour!*

Fifteens

15 marshmallows (combination of pink and white) finely chopped
15 red cherries, finely chopped
15 digestive biscuits, finely crushed
1 small tin Nestlé condensed milk
2 ounces coconut

In a bowl combine marshmallows, cherries, and crushed biscuits; mix well. Add condensed milk and mix until thoroughly blended.

Divide mixture into two even amounts and roll each into a log shape. Roll logs in coconut and chill in refrigerator for at least 2 hours.

Cut into slices and serve.

Chocolate Coconut Balls

10 digestive biscuits, finely crushed
2 ounces cocoa
2 ounces coconut
2 ounces butter
1 small tin Nestlé condensed milk

Melt butter and mix with milk. Add biscuit crumbs, coconut and cocoa. Shape into balls, roll in coconut, and chill in refrigerator.

Philip's Favorite Chocolate Cake

6 ounces self-rising flour, sifted
4 ounces butter, softened
5 ounces sugar
2 ounces cocoa, sifted with flour
3 large eggs
1–2 tablespoons water (if needed)

Cream butter and sugar until pale in color. Add eggs one at a time mixing thoroughly after each addition. Add flour and cocoa alternately with water until mixture forms a soft consistency when dropped from spoon.

Divide batter evenly between two 8 inch cake pans and bake at 375° for 20–25 minutes.

FILLING

2 ounces milk chocolate
2 ounces powdered sugar
2 ounces butter
1 tablespoon milk

Place chocolate and milk in small saucepan and heat gradually until chocolate has melted. Pour over combined butter and powdered sugar and whisk quickly until smooth. Spread smoothly until cake is covered.

Dedicated to my favorite brother.

"If we could give every individual the right amount
of nourishment and exercise, not too little and not too much,
we would have found the safest way to health."

HIPPOCRATES

Appetizers and Dips

Oven Roasted Red Peppers with Garlic & Olive Oil

4 large red peppers
1 teaspoon fresh chopped garlic (or substitute with garlic powder)
¼ cup olive oil
Salt and pepper

Preheat oven to broil. Wash peppers thoroughly, cut in half; remove seeds, and place skin side up on baking sheet. Broil peppers in oven until skin is blackened (about 15 minutes). Allow to cool. Peel blackened skin from peppers and discard. Cut peppers into 1 inch strips. Place peppers on serving dish, sprinkle with fresh garlic (or garlic powder), and salt and pepper to taste. Pour olive oil over peppers – place in refrigerator for 30 minutes to chill. Serve with thinly sliced French bread.

NOTE: Do not refrigerate peppers for longer than 30 minutes, as this will solidify the olive oil.

Stuffed Portobello Mushrooms

8 large Portobello mushrooms, washed and wiped dry
½ cup red pepper, finely chopped
½ cup yellow pepper, finely chopped
½ cup red onion, finely chopped
½ cup Italian breadcrumbs
½ cup Parmesan cheese, grated
½ cup lump crab meat, flaked, (optional)
2 cloves garlic, minced
Salt and pepper
4 tablespoons olive oil
1 jar marinara sauce

Remove stems from mushrooms and scoop out insides; chop finely. Heat olive oil in skillet and add mushroom stems, red pepper, yellow pepper, and red onion. Cook on medium heat until tender. Add garlic, salt and pepper. Cook 1 minute. Allow to cool. (Can be prepared one day head and placed in refrigerator.)

Stir in breadcrumbs, cheese and crab (if desired) to cooled mushroom mixture. Brush cookie sheet with a little olive oil. Spoon combined mixture into mushroom caps and top with tablespoon of marinara sauce. Bake for 15 minutes in 400° oven.

Heat remaining marinara sauce and spoon over top of stuffed mushrooms.

Serve immediately.

Hot Artichoke Dip

1 cup mayonnaise
1 cup sour cream
1 8-ounce packet cream cheese, softened
1 12-ounce jar marinated artichoke hearts, drained and roughly chopped
¼ cup shredded Parmesan cheese
Salt and pepper
1 teaspoon dill

Place mayonnaise, sour cream and cream cheese in bowl. Beat on medium speed until thoroughly blended. Stir in artichokes, cheese and salt and pepper. Place mixture in 9 x 12 glass dish. Sprinkle lightly with dill.

Bake in 350° oven for 15–20 minutes until bubbly and hot. Serve with thinly sliced French bread or tortilla chips.

Crab Dip

1 8-ounce packet cream cheese, softened
1 tablespoon milk
1/4 teaspoon white horseradish
Salt and pepper
6½ ounces lump crabmeat
2 tablespoons finely chopped onion

Blend first 4 ingredients together. Gently stir in crabmeat. Place in oven safe dish not deeper than 1 inch. Bake for 15 minutes at 375°.

Serve immediately with potato chips or lightly toasted French bread rounds.

Krispy Cheesettes

1 cup cheddar cheese, grated
2 cups unsweetened rice puffed cereal
2 cups butter
2 cups all purpose flour

Cream butter. Add cheese and flour and stir in cereal. Roll into small balls and flatten with a fork.

Bake for 10 minutes in 350°–375° oven. Cool and serve.

Cheese Fondue

3 cups grated Swiss cheese
1 cup grated Gruyère cheese
3 tablespoons all-purpose flour
1 clove garlic, peeled and cut in half
1½ cups dry white wine
1 tablespoon fresh lemon juice
White pepper to taste
2 tablespoons brandy or cognac
1 long loaf French bread, cut into thick slices and quartered

Toss grated cheese with flour and set aside. Rub inside of fondue pot or chafing dish with cut side of garlic clove and discard garlic. Heat fondue pot over medium heat on stovetop. Heat wine and lemon juice until hot, but not boiling. Maintaining medium heat, begin adding cheese by the handful, stirring clockwise constantly with a wooden spoon. Let each handful of cheese melt and become thoroughly incorporated before adding more. Be sure heat is evenly distributed, otherwise cheese will coagulate in the center.

When all cheese has melted and mixture is smooth and creamy, season to taste with pepper and nutmeg. Add brandy. Transfer pot to fondue burner. French bread may now be dipped into the mixture. If fondue becomes too thick, add a little wine and stir until smooth.

Other suggested dippers:
Boiled new potatoes, broccoli, cauliflower, radishes, cherry tomatoes, mushrooms, apple and pear slices.

NOTE: May be used as a main course or an appetizer.

Low-Fat Vegetable Dip

1 pint low-fat mayonnaise
1 pound fat-free or low-fat cottage cheese
¼ to ½ cup onion, finely minced
½ teaspoon salt
¼ teaspoon hot pepper sauce
1 teaspoon garlic, finely minced
1½ tablespoons Worcestershire sauce
1 teaspoon caraway seeds
½ teaspoon celery seeds
1 teaspoon dry mustard
1 teaspoon ground black pepper, freshly ground

Mix all ingredients thoroughly with portable mixer, or with food processor. Do not purée or over beat. Serve with crudités: raw carrots, peppers, or celery.

Cheese Doodads with Hot Pepper Jelly

¾ cup grated sharp cheddar cheese
6 tablespoons butter, chilled and cut into small pieces
1 cup flour
½ pepper jelly (jam)
1 jalapeño chili pepper, minced

Preheat oven to 400°. Place cheese, butter and flour into food processor. Pulse 6–8 times until flour resembles coarse corn meal. Continue to process until dough forms a ball. Do not over-process! Chill mixture for 30 minutes.

Scoop heaping teaspoons of cheese mixture, and roll into balls. Place balls in rows on baking sheet. Bake for 5 minutes or until balls begin to turn golden yellow. Remove cheese balls from oven and press center of each ball to form a dimple. Mix pepper jelly with minced jalapeño chili pepper. Spoon ¼ teaspoon jelly into each cheese ball dimple. Bake 6–8 minutes until golden brown.

NOTE: Doodads will cook more evenly if tray is rotated during baking.

Jacki's Salsa & Guacamole

SALSA

6 tomatoes, finely chopped, or pulsed in the food processor
½ sweet onion, finely chopped
2 tablespoons fresh cilantro, finely chopped
1 clove of garlic, finely chopped
Juice of one fresh lime
Dash Tabasco Sauce, to taste
Salt and white pepper, to taste

Put all ingredients in a bowl and mix together. Chill in refrigerator at least 2 hours – best chilled overnight. Serve with tortilla chips.

GUACAMOLE

8 ripe avocados, pitted and skins removed
½ sweet onion, finely chopped
2–3 tablespoons cilantro, finely chopped
Juice of 2 fresh limes
1 tomato, finely chopped
1 clove garlic, finely chopped
Dash Tabasco Sauce, to taste
Salt and pepper, to taste

Place avocados in a bowl and mash with a fork until smooth. Add remaining ingredients and mix together. Cover with plastic wrap to prevent avocados browning, and chill in refrigerator 2 hours. Serve with tortilla chips.

NOTE: These recipes are prepared mild. If you would like to make them hotter, simply add more Tabasco Sauce.

Contributed by Jacki Gass

Left to right: My sister-in-law Ruth, brother-in-law Neil, Ruth's husband Bill, Bob's uncle Vivian and his wife Barbara enjoy a meal in our home. (They licked the plates clean!)

Soups, Salads and Side Dishes

Quick Chicken & Corn Chowder

2 tablespoons olive oil
4 scallions, thinly sliced
1 green bell pepper, cut into ½ inch squares
½ pound red-skinned potatoes, unpeeled and diced
3 tablespoons flour
1 cup chicken broth
½ teaspoon salt
¼ teaspoon cayenne pepper
¼ teaspoon dried thyme
1 can (14¾ ounce) creamed corn
1½ cups chicken breasts, diced and cooked
½ cup heavy cream

In large saucepan, heat oil over medium heat. Add scallions, bell pepper, and potatoes and cook 5 minutes or until bell pepper is crisp-tender. Add flour, stirring to coat. Stir in broth, salt, cayenne, thyme, and 1 cup of water and bring to a boil. Reduce to simmer; cover and cook 5 minutes or until potatoes are tender. Stir in creamed corn, chicken and cream and bring to a boil. Serve immediately.

NOTE: To reduce the fat content in this recipe, reduce oil to 1 tablespoon in step 1 and use a nonstick saucepan. Use evaporated milk in place of heavy cream in step 2.

Pasta e Fagioli

2 tablespoons olive oil
2 medium onions, chopped
2–3 sticks celery, chopped
2 cloves garlic, minced
1 tablespoon basil
2 teaspoons oregano
2 cups chicken stock
⅓ cup sherry
1 can plum tomatoes
2 cans kidney beans
1 cup fusilli pasta
Salt and pepper
½ cup grated Parmesan cheese
1 medium zucchini, chopped
1 cup fresh green beans

Heat the oil in a 4-quart saucepan over medium heat and add the onion. Sauté until softened (about 5 minutes) and then add celery, garlic, basil, and oregano. Stir for a couple of minutes.

Add broth and bring to a boil, reduce heat and simmer about 5–10 minutes. Add the sherry, zucchini, tomatoes, green beans, and pasta and simmer for an additional 15 minutes until the pasta is cooked.

Season with salt and pepper. Stir in Parmesan cheese just before serving.

Contributed by Ruth Halliday

She Crab Soup

1 tablespoon butter
2½ tablespoons cornstarch
2 tablespoons minced onion
Salt and pepper
3 stalks celery, diced
Dash lime juice
2½ cups rich milk (1 cup milk, ¾ cup heavy cream, ¾ cup water)
1⅓ cups lump crab meat, flaked
½ cup sherry

In a skillet melt butter and add cornstarch. Stir until smooth. Stir in onion, salt and pepper, celery, lime and 1 cup milk. Cook for 5 minutes.

Add the rest of the milk and heat thoroughly. Slowly stir in crab meat and add sherry and stir to combine. Serve immediately.

Potato Leek Soup

3 cups leeks, thinly sliced (white and light green parts only)
1 cup ham, diced
1 clove garlic, minced
3 tablespoons butter
4 cups chicken broth
4 cups cabbage, coarsely sliced
4 cups potatoes, peeled and diced
1 bay leaf
1 cup heavy cream
Salt and pepper
4 tablespoons fresh chives, chopped

Cook leeks, ham, and garlic in butter in stockpot over medium heat until leeks are tender (approximately 10 minutes). Stir in broth, cabbage, potatoes and bay leaf. Simmer 30 minutes until potatoes are tender.

Stir in cream; continue to simmer until heated through. Season with salt and pepper to taste. Garnish individual servings with chopped fresh chives.

Contributed by Ruth Halliday

Red Bell Pepper & Tomato Soup

1 tablespoon olive oil
1 large onion, finely chopped
2 cloves garlic, finely chopped
3 tablespoons dry sherry
4 red bell peppers, de-seeded and chopped
1 potato, diced
2 large tomatoes, peeled and chopped
4½ cups chicken or vegetable stock
¼ cup fresh basil, finely chopped
½ cup heavy cream
Salt and pepper to taste

Heat oil in large saucepan and fry onions until tender. Add all ingredients except heavy cream and bring to a boil. Reduce heat and simmer covered for 30 minutes.

Allow mixture to cool. Place soup in a blender and purée until smooth. Stir in heavy cream and reheat slowly. Sprinkle with some additional chopped basil and serve.

NOTE: To lower the fat content in this recipe, substitute ½ cup low-fat evaporated milk for the ½ cup heavy cream.

Chicken Salad

3 cups cooked chicken breasts, cubed
1 tablespoon red onion, minced
Salt and pepper
2 tablespoons lemon juice
1 cup celery, finely chopped

(NOTE: Above may be prepared ahead.)

Toss with the following:

1 cup white grapes
⅓ cup mayonnaise (low-fat)
1 11-ounce can mandarin oranges
½ cup toasted almonds, slivered
2 tablespoons sour cream

After mixing, arrange salad on lettuce leaves and garnish with a few grapes and orange slices.

Wild Rice Salad

1 cup wild rice
1¼ cups chicken broth
1 clove garlic, finely chopped
1 bunch scallions, chopped
3 tablespoons butter
1 cup mushrooms, chopped
3 thin slices prosciutto or ham, julienned
½ cup black olives, chopped
2 tablespoons olive oil
3 tablespoons white wine vinegar with tarragon
½ teaspoon dried marjoram
Salt and pepper to taste

Soak rice in cold water for 2 hours. Rinse the rice and pour into pot with chicken broth and garlic. Cover and cook on low until all liquid is absorbed (about 25 minutes). Discard garlic. Rice should be dry, yet fluffy. In a medium-sized skillet, sauté the scallions in the butter until soft. Add mushrooms and toss briefly over high heat. Add onions and mushrooms to the rice along with the remaining ingredients. Toss well and season to taste with salt and pepper.

Chill, preferably 24 hours. Toss once more and serve cold.

NOTE: This recipe is also delicious served in tomato shells.

Mexicalli Summer Corn Salad

4 ears fresh white or yellow corn
1/3 cup green pepper, diced
1/3 cup sweet or red onion, diced
1 cup fresh tomato, diced
1 tablespoon jalapeño peppers, finely diced
4 ounces smoked Gouda cheese, cubed
2 tablespoons rice or apple cider vinegar
2 tablespoons lemon juice
3–4 tablespoons vegetable oil
1 teaspoon chili powder
1/2 teaspoon salt

Use sharp serrated knife to remove kernels of uncooked corn from ears. To a bowl add the next 5 ingredients and mix well.

Combine vinegar, lemon juice, oil, chili, and salt. Mix well.

Add liquid to first mixture, stir well and refrigerate 2 hours.

NOTE: This recipe may be prepared ahead and chilled overnight.

Contributed by Kathy Shea

Curried Chicken Salad

2 pounds cooked chicken breasts, skinless and boneless
6 ounces seedless grapes, halved
4 cups mixed salad leaves (e.g. romaine, red oak leaf, arugula)
Salt and pepper
Sprigs of fresh cilantro, to garnish

FOR THE DRESSING:

6 tablespoons low-fat mayonnaise
1 tablespoon medium-hot curry paste
1–2 tablespoons mango chutney

Shred the chicken breasts into bite-size pieces and place in a bowl with the grapes. Season to taste. Tear the salad leaves into bite-size pieces and arrange to form a bed on a serving platter or on individual plates.

Mix all the dressing ingredients together, adding just enough cold water to give dressing a pourable consistency. Combine and toss the chicken and the dressing. Place the chicken mixture on the salad and garnish with cilantro.

Asparagus Vinaigrette

2 pounds asparagus
1 cup canola oil
¼ cup balsamic vinegar
2 teaspoons Dijon mustard
2 cloves garlic, finely minced
½ teaspoon sugar

Steam asparagus until bright green; immediately rinse with ice water to retain color. Drain. Mix vinegar, mustard, garlic, and sugar and slowly whisk in oil. Pour mixture over asparagus and marinate for at least 4 hours, preferably overnight.

Serve chilled asparagus on a bed of lettuce.

My "wee" brother Philip, his fiancee Cheryl and I enjoy a cup of tea.

Spanakopita

2 tablespoons olive oil
1 onion, chopped
2 pounds fresh spinach
1 teaspoon dry oregano
8 ounces feta cheese, crumbled
4 eggs, beaten
Grated nutmeg
12 ounces filo pastry dough, thawed
¼ cup melted butter
Salt and pepper

Wash the spinach, shake to dry and place in a large boiler. Cover and cook for 8 minutes, shaking occasionally, until tender. Drain well, pressing out as much water as possible, then chop finely. Heat the oil and fry the onion for 4–5 minutes, until soft. Add the spinach, oregano, feta cheese, eggs and nutmeg. Season to taste and mix well.

Butter a shallow ovenproof dish, about 10 x 7 inches. Layer the filo dough in the dish, brushing each layer with melted butter. Reserve 3 filo sheets. Fill the filo crust with the spinach mixture. Fold over the dough edges, covering the filling. Cover with the remaining 3 filo sheets, tucking them in to fit the top, and brush with more melted butter. Place in a preheated oven, 375° for 45–50 minutes, until the dough is crisp and golden.

Tomato, Spinach & Ricotta Casserole

1½ pounds spinach, shredded (fresh or frozen)
2 tablespoons butter
1 onion, chopped
1 garlic clove, crushed
2 large tomatoes, peeled and sliced
12 ounces Ricotta cheese
2 tablespoons Parmesan cheese, grated
Salt and pepper

Place the spinach in a large saucepan with 1 tablespoon of water and a little salt. Cook for 2–3 minutes until soft, and then drain the spinach well. Melt the remaining butter in a saucepan. Add the onion and garlic, and cook until soft; then mix with the spinach.

Layer half the spinach, sliced tomatoes, and Ricotta cheese in an oiled casserole. Repeat the layers, seasoning each layer with salt and pepper. Sprinkle Parmesan cheese over the top.

Cover and place in a pre-heated oven at 350° for 30 minutes. Remove the lid and cook for 10 minutes longer to brown.

Zucchini Casserole

1½ pounds zucchini, roughly chopped
1 onion, chopped
2 garlic cloves, crushed
5 tablespoons olive oil
½ cup long-grain rice
2 eggs
Salt and pepper
½ cup Gruyère cheese, grated
3–4 tablespoons fresh breadcrumbs
2 tablespoons Parmesan cheese, grated

In a large skillet fry the zucchini, onion, and garlic slowly in 3 tablespoons olive oil until soft and slightly golden. Meanwhile, cook the rice in a large saucepan of boiling salted water. Rice should be tender but not sticky when done. Drain well.

Beat the eggs with salt and pepper in a large bowl, and then stir in the cooked zucchini mixture, grated Gruyère cheese, and drained rice. Transfer to an oiled, shallow ovenproof dish. Sprinkle zucchini mixture with breadcrumbs and Parmesan cheese and drizzle the remaining olive oil over the top. Place in a preheated oven at 350° for 20–30 minutes, until crisp and golden brown. Serve casserole hot or chilled.

Potato Cakes

2 pounds potatoes
3 eggs
⅔ cup onions, finely chopped
1 tablespoon all-purpose flour
1 tablespoon fresh parsley and chives, finely chopped
1 garlic clove, minced
Nutmeg, freshly grated
6 tablespoons oil
Salt and pepper

Grate the potatoes coarsely. Place potatoes in a strainer and rinse under cold running water. Drain and transfer the potatoes to a bowl.

Add the eggs to the bowl of grated potatoes and mix well. Stir in the onions, flour, parsley, chives, and garlic. Season with salt, pepper, and grated nutmeg and then stir the mixture thoroughly. Divide the potato mixture into equal-size portions and, using a spoon, mold them into small cakes.

Heat the oil in a skillet. When hot, add the potato cakes and fry until golden brown and crisp on both sides, turning them once during cooking. Serve with sour cream if desired.

Potatoes au Gratin

1 garlic clove, cut in half
⅓ cup butter, softened
2 pounds potatoes, peeled and thinly sliced
Nutmeg, freshly grated
1½ cups hot milk
1 cup light cream
Salt and pepper

Rub the cut garlic around the inside of a large earthenware baking dish, and then brush the dish thickly with some of the softened butter. Place a layer of the thinly sliced potatoes in the dish and sprinkle with salt, pepper and nutmeg. Continue layering the potatoes in this way, seasoning each layer. Mix the milk and cream, and then pour this mixture over the potatoes, so that they are almost covered by the liquid.

Dot the remaining butter over the top, then bake in a preheated oven, 350° for 1–1¼ hours, or until tender when pierced with a skewer. Increase the oven heat to 400° for the last 15 minutes of cooking time to brown the top layer.

Entrees

"Omit and substitute! That's how recipes should be written. Please don't ever get so hung up on published recipes that you forget to omit and substitute."

JEFF SMITH – THE FRUGAL GOURMET

Chicken

Chicken-Stuffed Manicotti with Porcini Cream Sauce

1 package (.35 ounce) Porcini mushrooms, dried
1 cup boiling water
16 manicotti shells
3 tablespoons olive oil
2 large onions, finely chopped
5 cloves garlic, finely chopped
2 pounds chicken breast, ground
1 cup heavy cream
1 teaspoon salt
¾ teaspoon black pepper, freshly ground
1 pound fresh Shiitake or regular mushrooms, stems trimmed and caps thinly sliced
¼ cup bourbon or brandy
¾ cup chicken broth
½ cup Parmesan cheese, grated

In small bowl, combine dried Porcini mushrooms and boiling water and let stand 20 minutes or until mushrooms are soft. Scoop out mushroom caps and rinse under running water. Coarsely chop; set aside. Strain liquid used to soak mushrooms and set aside. Meanwhile, in large pot of boiling water, cook manicotti shells according to package directions. Drain, rinse under running water, and set aside.

In large skillet, heat oil over medium heat. Add onions and garlic and cook for 5–7 minutes, stirring frequently. Transfer 1 cup of onion mixture to large bowl and cool to room temperature. Add to this mixture chicken, ¼ cup of cream, ¾ teaspoon of salt, ½ teaspoon of pepper, ½ teaspoon sage, and ⅓ cup of reserved mushroom-soaking liquid. Mix well. Preheat oven to 350°. Fill a pastry bag or large sturdy zip seal bag with chicken filling. Pipe into cooked manicotti shells. Place 8 manicotti shells in each of two 9 x 13 inch baking dishes.

Heat skillet and add fresh Shiitakes and reconstituted Porcini, and cook, stirring frequently, 5 minutes or until fresh mushrooms are tender. Add bourbon, bring to boil, and cook 1 minute to evaporate alcohol. Add broth and remaining reserved mushroom-soaking liquid; bring to a boil and boil 3 minutes. Add remaining ¾ cup cream, ½ teaspoon salt, ¼ teaspoon pepper, and ¼ teaspoon sage; bring to a boil and boil 1 minute. Pour cream sauce over manicotti, cover, and bake for 30 minutes. Uncover, sprinkle with Parmesan cheese, and bake for another 10 minutes until golden brown.

Chicken Rolls Stuffed with Asparagus & Black Forest Ham

12 thin stalks asparagus
6 ounces Gorgonzola or other blue cheese
2 tablespoons cream cheese
$1/3$ cup pecan halves, finely chopped
$1/2$ teaspoon black pepper, freshly ground
4 small skinless, boneless chicken breasts, pounded to 1/4-inch thickness
$1/4$ pound Black Forest ham, thinly sliced
1 large egg
1 cup Italian breadcrumbs
2 tablespoons olive oil

In medium pot of boiling water, blanch asparagus for 2 minutes. Drain and rinse; place in ice water. In medium bowl, with electric mixer, beat Gorgonzola and cream cheese until well combined. Stir in pecans, pepper, and sage.

Place chicken cutlets on work surface, skinned side down, with one short end facing up. Cover entire surface of chicken with ham. Spread cheese mixture to within $1/2$ inch of each short end. Place 3 asparagus spears crosswise and roll chicken up from one short end. Secure roll with toothpicks. Preheat over to 400°. In shallow bowl or pie plate, beat egg with 1 tablespoon of water. In another shallow bowl, toss together bread crumbs and oil. Dip each chicken roll in egg mixture. Then dip in bread crumb mixture, patting crumbs into the roll. Place chicken rolls, seam-side down, on lightly greased baking sheet and bake for 25 minutes or until topping is golden and chicken is firm to the touch. Remove toothpicks before serving.

NOTE: To reduce the fat in this recipe reduce Gorgonzola cheese to 3 ounces and use 4 tablespoons reduced-fat cream cheese (Neufchatel) instead of regular cream cheese. Reduce amount of pecans to $1/4$ cup. Omit the oil and spray chicken rolls lightly with nonstick cooking spray before baking.

Chicken-Jack Enchiladas with Salsa Verde

3 tablespoons olive oil
1 small onion, finely chopped
2 cloves garlic, minced
2 cups chicken breasts, shredded and cooked
1 can (4$\frac{1}{2}$ ounces) mild green chili peppers, chopped
$\frac{1}{3}$ cup cilantro, chopped
1 jalapeño pepper, finely minced
$\frac{1}{4}$ teaspoon salt
1 12-ounce jar salsa
$\frac{1}{3}$ cup heavy cream
8 corn tortillas (6-inch diameter)
6 ounces Monterey Jack or Cheddar cheese, shredded

In small skillet, heat 1 tablespoon of oil over low heat. Add onion and garlic, and cook 7 minutes or until onion is tender. Stir in chicken, mild green chili peppers, cilantro, jalapeños, and salt. Stir until combined. In small bowl, combine salsa and cream. Preheat oven to 350°. In large skillet, heat remaining 2 tablespoons oil. Gently heat each tortilla in oil for 5 seconds. Drain on paper towels. Dip each tortilla in salsa mixture. Dividing evenly, spoon chicken filling down center of tortillas. Top each tortilla with 1 tablespoon of Monterey Jack cheese and roll enchiladas.

Spread $\frac{1}{3}$ cup of salsa mixture onto bottom of 7 x 11-inch glass baking dish. Place enchiladas, seam-side down, in dish. Pour remaining salsa on top. Cover with foil and bake for 20 minutes or until piping hot. Uncover, sprinkle remaining 1 cup Monterey Jack cheese on top, and bake for 5 minutes or until cheese is melted.

NOTE: To reduce the fat in this recipe, omit 2 tablespoons oil when sautéing the tortillas. Instead, to soften tortillas for rolling, wrap in foil and heat in 250° oven for 10 minutes. Cheese may also be reduced to 1 cup.

Chicken Pot Pie

4 boneless skinless chicken breasts, cut into 1 inch cubes
1 small onion, roughly chopped
1 can of Campbell's Cream of Chicken soup, undiluted
1 can of Campbell's Cream of Mushroom soup, undiluted
1 bag frozen peas and carrots, thawed
1 bag frozen broccoli, thawed and roughly chopped
2 large potatoes, peeled, cubed and boiled.
¼ cup white cooking wine
¼ cup milk or cream
1 packet frozen puff pastry sheets, thawed
2 tablespoons olive oil
1 teaspoon fresh garlic, chopped
Salt and pepper

Heat 1 tablespoon of olive oil in large skillet. Add onion and cook until glazed and tender. Stir in garlic and cook gently about 1 minute. Add remaining olive oil and chicken to skillet and cook until chicken is thoroughly done.

To skillet add soups, frozen peas and carrots, broccoli, potatoes, white wine and salt and pepper to taste. Bring mixture to a boil and allow to simmer for 3 minutes. Remove from heat. Slowly stir in milk or cream. Allow to cool.

Heat oven to 425°. Roll out one puff pastry sheet into 9 x 13 rectangle. Place all ingredients into 9 x 13 baking dish. Place puff pastry on top. Brush with beaten egg and bake at 425° for 30 minutes. Serve immediately.

Contributed by Susan Hill

Chicken Stuffed with Roasted Red Peppers & Cream Cheese

6 boneless, skinless chicken breasts
4 red peppers, blackened with skins removed (see recipe on page 12)
8 ounces cream cheese, softened
Salt and pepper
Garlic powder
1 cup Italian breadcrumbs
2 tablespoons olive oil

Cover chicken breasts with plastic wrap and gently pound until ¼ inch thick. Place smooth side down and wipe off excess moisture with paper towel. Season cream cheese with garlic powder, and add salt and pepper to taste. Spread approximately 1 tablespoon of cream cheese mixture onto chicken breast, place 3 roasted red pepper slices on top and sprinkle with some additional salt, pepper, and garlic powder. Gently roll up and secure with toothpick. Repeat for each chicken breast. Place in lightly greased ovenproof dish – do not cover.

Mix breadcrumbs and olive oil thoroughly. Sprinkle each chicken breast with breadcrumb mixture and press gently into breast meat.

Bake in 375° oven for 25–30 minutes.

NOTE: This dish may be served hot or cold with tossed salad greens.

Tarragon Chicken with Angel Hair Pasta

6 boneless chicken breast halves
3 tablespoons butter
2 cloves garlic, minced
1 teaspoon dried whole tarragon, crumbled
1 cup heavy cream
¾ cup grated Parmesan cheese
¼ teaspoon salt
½ cup dry white wine
¼ teaspoon cayenne pepper
1 pound angel hair pasta, cooked

Lightly pound chicken breast halves between pieces of waxed paper. Sauté chicken in butter over medium-high heat, about 1 minute on each side. Add garlic, tarragon, cream, Parmesan cheese, salt, wine, and cayenne pepper. Stir until blended; cook over medium heat until chicken is done and sauce is slightly reduced, about 15 minutes.

Serve chicken over angel hair pasta.

Chicken Artichoke Casserole

1 cup butter
½ cup all-purpose flour
3½ cups milk
¼ teaspoon cayenne pepper
1 clove garlic, minced
1 cup sharp Cheddar cheese, grated
1 (10-ounce) can button mushrooms, drained
8 boneless chicken breast halves, cooked and cut into bite-size pieces
2 (14-ounce) cans artichoke hearts, drained and quartered
2 cups fresh bread crumbs
4 tablespoons butter, melted

Melt butter in saucepan; stir in flour and cook over low heat for 5–10 minutes until lightly browned. Gradually add milk and stir until thick and smooth. Stir in cayenne pepper, garlic, and cheese and stir until cheese melts and mixture bubbles. Add mushrooms. Arrange chicken in greased 13 x 9 x 2 inch casserole dish and top with artichokes and sauce. Mix bread crumbs with butter; sprinkle over dish. Bake at 350° for 30 minutes.

NOTE: Casserole may be prepared ahead and baked just before serving. Great for a crowd!

Pecan Crusted Chicken Breasts with Brandy Cream Sauce

6 chicken breasts, boneless, skinless
2 cups pecans, finely crushed or pulsed in food processor
4 tablespoons flour, seasoned
1 egg, lightly beaten with 3 tablespoons water added to make egg wash
8 ounces butter
½ cup brandy
1 cup heavy cream
2 teaspoons flour
Salt and white pepper

Trim all fat from chicken breasts. Pound lightly. Dip chicken in egg wash, seasoned flour and again in egg wash. Coat generously with pecan crumbs.

Melt half of butter in pan over medium heat and add chicken, gently sauté until pecan crust is golden brown, being careful not to burn (about 5 minutes). Turn and cook another 5 minutes until chicken is evenly browned. Carefully transfer chicken to greased oven safe dish. Bake in 400° oven for 25 minutes.

Melt remaining butter in pan over medium heat and add flour to make roux. Add brandy and bring to a rapid boil, stirring frequently with a small whisk until slightly reduced and smooth. Add heavy cream, salt and white pepper. Continue stirring until sauce has reduced and thickened. (If sauce is too thick, add extra cream).

Pour sauce over prepared chicken and serve.

Meats

Filet Mignon with Fresh Mushroom Cream Sauce

6 6-ounce filet mignons
6 slices of white bread, crusts removed and trimmed to size of filets
12 tablespoons butter, divided
1 pound fresh mushrooms, sliced
2 teaspoons all-purpose flour
1 cup heavy cream, heated
½ cup brandy
Salt and pepper to taste
Fresh parsley sprigs for garnish

In skillet, sauté filets in 3 tablespoons butter for 4 minutes on each side. (Filets may also be grilled). Remove cooked filets; keep warm.

In same skillet, sauté mushrooms in 3 tablespoons butter; add flour, salt and pepper. Blend well. Stir in warm cream, do not boil. Add brandy to mushroom sauce and heat thoroughly.

Meanwhile, sauté bread slices in 6 tablespoons butter. Arrange bread slices on platter; top each with a cooked filet. Spoon sauce over meat. Garnish with fresh parsley. Serve meat with additional sauce at table.

Homemade Spaghetti Sauce & Meatballs

SPAGHETTI SAUCE

3 28-ounce cans of diced or crushed tomatoes
2 8-ounce cans tomato sauce
1 small onion, finely chopped
8 cloves of garlic, finely chopped
½ cup fresh parsley washed, stems removed, and finely chopped
¼ cup fresh oregano, finely chopped
¼ cup fresh basil leaves, finely chopped
½ cup of red wine
1 teaspoon sugar
Salt and pepper
Olive oil

Heat 2 tablespoons of olive oil in large pot, add onion and cook on medium heat until tender. Add garlic and stir until lightly browned. Add canned tomatoes, tomato sauce, parsley, oregano, basil, sugar, salt and pepper, and red wine. Mix together well. Cook for 2 hours on low heat, stirring frequently.

NOTE: This sauce is best prepared one day ahead, stored in the refrigerator overnight and then slowly reheated.

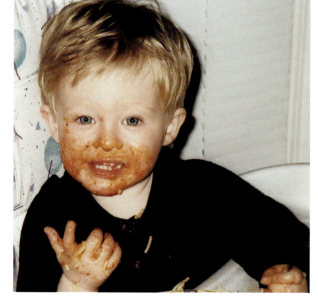

Grandson Alex enjoys some spaghetti and meatballs.

MEATBALLS

2 pounds lean ground beef
1 onion, finely chopped
4 large cloves of garlic, finely chopped
1 cup Italian breadcrumbs
1 teaspoon dried oregano
1 egg, lightly beaten
Salt and pepper
Olive oil

Place ground beef in large mixing bowl and add onion, garlic, dried oregano and salt and pepper. Mix ingredients together well. Add half of breadcrumbs and mix well, then add remaining breadcrumbs. Add lightly beaten egg and continue to mix well until absorbed into meat mixture. Roll mixture into balls about 2 inches in diameter.

Heat ¼ cup olive oil in skillet. Add meatballs (be careful not to over-crowd pan) and cook on medium heat until browned. Place meatballs in ovenproof dish, spoon generous amount of spaghetti sauce over the top, cover with foil and bake in 350° oven for 25 minutes.

Cook entire package of spaghetti according to directions. Drain and serve immediately, topped with meatballs and sauce.

NOTE: Delicious served with garlic bread and tossed salad.

Steak Fajitas

1 pound boneless sirloin steak, cut into ¼ inch strips
1 medium onion, thinly sliced
1 green pepper, thinly sliced
1 red pepper, thinly sliced
2 tablespoons olive oil, divided
1 fresh lime
8 medium flour tortillas
½ cup cheddar cheese, shredded
1 12-ounce jar of salsa
½ cup low-fat sour cream

MARINADE

¼ cup orange juice
¼ cup fresh lime juice
¼ cup white vinegar
4 cloves garlic, minced
½ teaspoon seasoned salt
Dash cayenne pepper, to taste

In a large resealable plastic bag, combine marinade ingredients; add beef strips. Seal bag, turn to coat, and place in refrigerator for 2 hours.

In a skillet, sauté onion and peppers in oil until crisp tender; remove and set aside. Drain beef strips and discard marinade, cook beef in remaining oil on high heat to desired doneness. Return vegetables to pan; heat through. Just before serving, squeeze juice of lime over meat/vegetable mixture. Warm tortillas in 350° oven for 5 minutes. Spoon meat/vegetables onto tortillas. Top with shredded cheese, salsa, and sour cream.

Cheryl's "Ultra-Quick" Lasagna

1 pound uncooked lasagna
1 12-ounce packet mozzarella cheese
(about 3 cups), shredded

SAUCE
1 32-ounce jar tomato sauce
1 garlic clove, minced
1 cup dry red wine
1 tablespoon fresh oregano
1 tablespoon fresh parsley flakes
1 tablespoon fresh basil
1 teaspoon fresh rosemary
1 teaspoon garlic salt
Combine all ingredients in large bowl.

CHEESE FILLING
2 eggs, beaten
2 cups part-skim (or fat free) ricotta cheese
1/3 cup Parmesan cheese, grated
1/4 teaspoon nutmeg
Combine all ingredients in separate bowl.

MEAT FILLING
1 pound ground turkey (can also use beef)
1 large onion, finely chopped
2 tablespoons olive oil
1/2 tablespoon garlic, finely chopped

To prepare the meat filling, heat oil in large skillet over medium heat; add garlic and onions and cook until garlic is just brown and onions are tender (approximately 3-5 minutes). Add turkey and cook until brown.

Pour a generous amount of the sauce mixture in bottom of 9 x 13 inch pan; alternate layers of uncooked lasagna, sauce, meat mixture, ricotta mixture, and top with mozzarella cheese. Repeat for 2–3 layers, ending with mozzarella. (The pasta will cook in the sauce, resulting in tender pasta layers.)

Cover with foil and bake 1 hour at 350°; remove foil and bake for 15 more minutes. Let stand for 10 minutes before serving.

NOTE: This recipe can be prepared up to 24 hours in advance and stored in the refrigerator. Simply bring to room temperature before cooking.

Contributed by Cheryl Halliday

Pot Roast in a Bag

2 pounds bottom round or rump roast, trimmed
Juice of 1 lemon
2 onions, thinly sliced
20 baby carrots
2 potatoes, peeled and quartered
2 stalks of celery, sliced
1 red bell pepper, roughly chopped
3 cloves of garlic, finely chopped
1 teaspoon dry mustard
1 teaspoon dry thyme
1 8-ounce can tomato sauce
1 cup of water
¼ cup red cooking wine
1 oven cooking bag

Place beef in shallow roasting pan. Sprinkle beef with lemon juice; pierce with a fork. Cover and refrigerate until ready to use.

Preheat oven to 350°. Place beef in cooking bag and return to roasting pan. Arrange onions, carrots, and potatoes around beef. Top with celery and bell pepper. Sprinkle beef with mustard, garlic, and thyme. Mix tomato sauce with wine and 1 cup of water, pour around beef. Seal cooking bag; cut slits in bag and roast for 1½ hours until very tender.

Remove beef from cooking bag; allow to stand for 5 minutes. Cut into slices and arrange vegetables around beef on serving platter.

NOTE: To serve this dish with gravy, substitute 3 bouillon cubes, 2 cups hot water and 1 tablespoon cornstarch for the tomato sauce. Mix well and pour around beef in bag. Mixture will form a thick gravy while roasting in oven.

Greek Shepherd's Pie

4 large potatoes, peeled and cubed
½ cup low-fat sour cream
¼ cup butter
5½ cups eggplant, peeled and cubed
  (about 1 large eggplant)
2 teaspoons salt
1 pound ground lamb (may use ground beef)
½ pound lean ground turkey
1 jar meatless spaghetti sauce

4 ounces feta cheese, crumbled
1 small onion, finely chopped
2 tablespoons fresh parsley, minced
1 teaspoon garlic powder
½ teaspoon dried rosemary, crushed
½ teaspoon dried basil
2 tablespoons all-purpose flour
¼ cup olive oil
Salt and pepper to taste

In a large saucepan, cook potatoes in boiling water until tender, then drain. Mash potatoes with sour cream, butter, and salt and pepper to taste; set aside. In a bowl, combine eggplant and salt. Let stand for 10 minutes, then wash and drain. Add flour and coat the eggplant. In a skillet, cook eggplant in oil over medium heat until browned. Transfer to a greased 3-quart baking dish.

In the same skillet, add a little extra oil and cook onions until tender. Add lamb and turkey and cook over medium heat until browned. Stir in spaghetti sauce, parsley, seasoning and salt and pepper to taste. Cook until heated through (about 5 minutes). Pour sauce mixture over eggplant, sprinkle with feta cheese and spread mashed potatoes over the top.

Bake uncovered at 350° for 45 minutes or until top begins to brown. Let stand for 10 minutes before serving.

NOTE: This recipe is a wonderful variation on an old favorite.

Pork Chops Stuffed with Apricots

6 rib pork chops, 1 inch thick
2 12-ounce cans apricot halves
½ cup ketchup
4 tablespoons olive oil
2 tablespoons lemon juice
1 teaspoon dry mustard
4 tablespoons onions, chopped
Salt and pepper

Cut pocket in pork chops and season inside with salt and pepper. Drain apricots, reserving 1 cup of liquid. Place 2 apricot halves in each pocket of pork chops. Dice remaining fruit and set aside. Grill chops over medium coals for 25–30 minutes, turning once.

In a saucepan combine the ketchup, oil, lemon juice, dry mustard, onions, diced apricots and reserved liquid. Bring mixture to a boil, reduce heat and simmer for 15 minutes until sauce has thickened. Brush chops with sauce and cook for another 5 minutes. Serve with apricot sauce on the side.

Contributed by Tom Lissak

Pork Paprika

1 pound pork tenderloin, cut into 1 inch pieces (may use chicken)
¼ pound mushrooms, washed and sliced
1 onion, thinly sliced
1 12-ounce tin of tomatoes
¼ pound frozen garden peas
1 tablespoon paprika
2 tablespoons sherry
1 bay leaf
2 tablespoons seasoned flour
2 tablespoons butter
Salt and pepper to taste

Toss pork in seasoned flour and gently sauté in 1 tablespoon butter until browned. Add remaining butter and the onion to pan and cook until tender and glazed. Place pork and onion in casserole dish and set aside. Simmer tomatoes, peas, paprika, bay leaf and salt and pepper in saucepan until flavors are well blended. Pour sauce over meat and cook in 350° oven for 30 minutes. Add sliced mushrooms and sherry and cook for an additional 15 minutes. Serve over rice.

Veal Marsala

2 pounds veal cutlets, pounded thin
8 ounces mushrooms, cleaned and thinly sliced
½ cup Marsala cooking wine
4 ounces butter
¾ cup heavy cream
Olive oil
Salt and pepper
6 tablespoons flour, seasoned with salt and pepper

Dredge veal in seasoned flour and set aside. In a sauté pan, heat 2 ounces butter and a little olive oil. Add half of veal and cook on high heat approximately 2 minutes each side. Remove and keep veal warm in oven. Repeat process with remaining veal.

Place mushrooms in sauté pan (add more butter/olive oil if needed) and cook until just tender. Add Marsala wine, salt and pepper to taste and bring to rapid boil. Mixture will begin to thicken and reduce. Lower heat and add cream. Return veal to pan and simmer for 1–2 minutes. Serve immediately.

NOTE: This dish is delicious served with herb roasted baby potatoes or angel hair pasta.

Lamb Curry

2 cups cooked lamb, cubed
1 medium onion, chopped
½ green pepper, finely chopped
1 small stalk celery, finely chopped
1 apple, thinly sliced
¼ cup butter
¼ cup all purpose flour
2 teaspoons curry powder, mild or hot
2 cups chicken broth
½ teaspoon salt
Olive oil
¼ cup heavy cream
3 cups hot cooked rice
½ cup chutney

Melt butter in saucepan and add onions, green pepper, celery and apple; cook until tender. Blend in flour, curry powder and salt. Stir over low heat until mixture is hot and bubbly. Remove from heat. Gradually stir in chicken broth, bring to a boil and cook for 1 minute. Add lamb and cook gently for 30 minutes on low heat. Just before serving add heavy cream and mix well. Serve over rice and top with chutney.

Contributed by Tom Lissak

Fish

"Do not overcook fish. Most seafood … should be simply
threatened with heat and then celebrated with joy"
JEFF SMITH – THE FRUGAL GOURMET

Salmon Picatta

4 6-ounce salmon filets with skin
½ cup white wine
Juice of 1 large lemon
4 ounces butter, cut into pieces
½ cup heavy cream
1 teaspoon sugar
1 jar capers, drained
Salt and pepper
½ teaspoon dill (dried or fresh)

Wash and dry salmon. Place in lightly greased baking dish and season with salt, pepper, and dill. Bake in 425° oven for 12–15 minutes until opaque.

Pour wine and lemon juice into sauté pan and bring to a boil. Simmer until slightly reduced. Lower heat and add butter one piece at a time stirring until mixture begins to thicken. Add cream and salt and pepper to taste (if too bitter, add ½ to 1 teaspoon of sugar). Gently stir in capers. Place salmon in sauté pan and allow to simmer gently in sauce for 3 minutes. Serve immediately.

NOTE: This dish is delicious served with wild rice, roasted baby potatoes, or over angel hair pasta.

Penne with Salmon & Asparagus

2 cups penne pasta
1 chicken bouillon cube
½ cup dry white wine
1 pound asparagus, cut into 1-inch lengths
¾ pound salmon fillets, skinned and cut into 4 pieces
1 cup nonfat sour cream
2 tablespoons whole-grain mustard
¾ teaspoon salt
½ teaspoon pepper, freshly ground
4 tablespoons chives, chopped

Cook penne pasta according to package directions; drain and place in serving bowl. In a large skillet, bring ½ cup water to a boil. Add the bouillon cube; stir until dissolved, then add the wine. Add the asparagus and salmon; poach until the fish is just opaque in the center and the asparagus is tender crisp, (about 5–6 minutes). With a slotted spoon, transfer the salmon and asparagus to the serving bowl; reserve the cooking liquid. Flake the salmon into bite-sized pieces.

In a medium bowl, beat the sour cream, mustard, salt, pepper, 3 tablespoons of the chives and the cooking liquid. Pour over the penne mixture; toss to coat. Sprinkle with the remaining chives.

Contributed by Ginny Gass

Crab Cakes with Roasted Red Pepper Sauce

1½ pounds jumbo lump crab meat
½ large onion, finely diced
½ bunch green onions, diced
½ red bell pepper, diced
½ yellow bell pepper, diced
1 clove of garlic, minced
½ cup fresh parsley, finely chopped
¼ cup fresh basil, finely chopped

1 tablespoon garlic powder
½ teaspoon dried thyme
Salt and pepper
4 ounces butter
2 cups heavy cream
3 tablespoons flour
1 cup breadcrumbs
½ cup Dijon mustard

Melt 2 ounces butter and add onions, peppers, and garlic. Cook onion mixture until transparent. Add remaining butter and melt on low heat. Add flour. Mix well with butter and vegetables to make a light roux. Add cream, mustard, basil, garlic powder and thyme. Leave on low heat, stirring frequently until very thick. Cool the sauce to room temperature. Add crabmeat and breadcrumbs and shape into 4-ounce patties. Refrigerate at least 3 hours, preferably overnight. (Makes 16 cakes).

To cook: Place 3 tablespoons olive oil in pan, dip crab cakes lightly in flour and fry until golden brown.

SAUCE

4 red bell peppers
1 teaspoon garlic

Salt and pepper
1 cup whipping cream

Cut peppers in half lengthways, place on baking sheet and broil in oven until blackened. Allow to cool and remove skins and seeds.

Place peppers in food processor and purée until smooth. Add garlic and salt and pepper to taste. Add cream and pulse slowly until well mixed, being careful not to over-thicken cream. Heat on low and pour sauce over crab cakes.

Bourbon-Bacon Scallops

3 tablespoons green onions, minced
2 tablespoons bourbon
2 tablespoons maple syrup
1 tablespoon low-sodium soy sauce
1 tablespoon Dijon mustard
24 large sea scallops
6 slices low-fat bacon
Salt and pepper to taste

Combine first 5 ingredients in a bowl; stir well. Add scallops and coat with marinade. Cover and refrigerate 2 hours, stirring occasionally.

Remove scallops from bowl and reserve the marinade. Cut each bacon slice into 4 pieces and wrap one piece around each scallop. Thread scallops onto 12-inch wooden skewers, leaving some space between scallops so that they will cook evenly.

Place skewers on a broiler pan coated with cooking spray and broil for about 8 minutes until bacon is crisp; continue to brush with reserved marinade. Serve over rice pilaf.

NOTE: This is a delicious low-fat recipe.

Baked Parmesan Fish

6 6-ounce fish fillets (cod, haddock, or other white fish)
½ cup low-fat sour cream
3 tablespoons Parmesan cheese, grated
¼ teaspoon paprika
¼ teaspoon dried tarragon leaves
6 lemon slices
Salt and pepper to taste

Roll up fish fillets; place seam side down on lightly greased baking dish. Sprinkle fillets with salt and pepper. Mix together sour cream, cheese, paprika and tarragon. Spread evenly over fish fillets and bake in 350° oven for 20–25 minutes until fish flakes easily with fork.

Serve with lemon slices and tossed salad greens.

NOTE: This recipe is not only quick and easy, but also low in fat.

Spicy Shrimp Salad with Cool Mango Sauce

1 fresh mango
2 tablespoons lemon juice
1 pound large shrimp, peeled and deveined
1 tablespoon olive oil
1 tablespoon chicken stock
1 teaspoon chili powder
¼ teaspoon hot pepper sauce
1½ cups fresh pineapple, chopped
1 cup tomatoes, chopped
1 red onion, thinly sliced
¼ cup fresh mint, finely chopped
2 cups mixed salad greens

Peel the mango and cut flesh away from pit. Purée mango and lemon juice in a blender. Place mixture in refrigerator to chill. Heat oil in skillet over medium heat. Combine shrimp, chicken stock, chili powder and hot-pepper sauce. Cook until shrimp is pink and well coated with seasonings, about 3–4 minutes.

NOTE: Do not overcook shrimp – they will become rubbery.

Remove shrimp from heat and allow to cool. To the shrimp add pineapple, tomatoes, onions and mint. Place shrimp in refrigerator and chill at least 1 hour or until flavors are well blended. Spoon shrimp mixture over salad greens and drizzle with mango purée.

Thai Shrimp in Coconut Sauce

20 large uncooked shrimp, peeled and deveined
2 tablespoons olive oil
1 large onion, finely chopped
2 stalks of lemon grass, finely chopped (or 1 tablespoon lemon peel)
2 fresh red chili peppers, sliced
1 inch piece of fresh ginger, finely chopped
2 tablespoons fish sauce
1 tablespoon ground cumin
1 tablespoon ground coriander
1 cup coconut milk
3 tablespoons roasted peanuts, coarsely ground (optional)
2 tomatoes, peeled and finely chopped
1 teaspoon sugar
½ lime, juiced
Fresh cilantro leaves, chopped

Heat oil in wok or skillet; add onion and cook until soft. Add lemon grass, sliced red chili peppers, ginger, cumin, coriander, and sauté for 2 minutes.

Add fish sauce and coconut milk, stir well; add peanuts and chopped tomatoes. Cook over low heat until flavors are well developed (about 5 minutes). Stir in shrimp and simmer slowly for 5 minutes until shrimp are pink and tender. Add sugar and place in serving dish. Sprinkle with fresh lime juice and garnish with cilantro. Serve with steamed rice.

Desserts

*"The smell and taste of things remain poised a long time...
like souls, ready to remind us..."*

MARCEL PROUST

Grandmommie's Sour Cream Pound Cake

7 large eggs, separated
3½ cups plain flour
2½ cups sugar
2 sticks margarine
½ cup shortening
1 teaspoon baking powder

¼ teaspoon baking soda
½ teaspoon salt
1 cup sour cream
1 teaspoon vanilla
1 teaspoon almond extract

Beat egg whites until stiff. Add 6 tablespoons sugar, beat and set aside. Sift flour, baking powder, salt and soda together. Cream margarine, shortening, and sugar together until soft and fluffy. Add egg yolks one at a time beating well after each addition.

Add dry ingredients alternately with sour cream, beginning and ending with dry ingredients. Add almond and vanilla. Fold in beaten egg whites. Pour into greased and floured bundt pan or two loaf pans. Bake at 325° for 30 minutes. Reduce heat to 300° and continue baking another 45 minutes or until cake is done.

GLAZE

1 stick margarine
1 cup confectioner's sugar
3 tablespoons milk
¼ teaspoon almond flavoring
1 teaspoon vanilla

Melt margarine; add sugar and milk and stir until well mixed. Add flavoring and beat well. Drizzle over cake while it is still very hot.

NOTE: Cake is delicious with or without glaze.

Contributed by Virginia Hammond – "Grandmommie"

Raspberry and White Chocolate Bread Pudding

4 tablespoons unsalted butter, melted
4 large eggs, separated
1 cup light brown sugar
3 cups heavy cream
1 cup milk
1 teaspoon pure vanilla extract
½ teaspoon ground cinnamon
1 cup fresh raspberries
6 cups day-old French bread cubes (½ inch)
6 ounces white chocolate, chopped
Whipped cream
Powdered sugar in small shaker
Fresh mint sprigs

Brush a baking dish (10 x 14 inches) with 2 tablespoons of butter. In a large bowl, whisk together the eggs, brown sugar, cream, and milk. Add the vanilla, cinnamon, raspberries, bread and chocolate and blend thoroughly. Stir the remaining 2 tablespoons butter into the mixture and pour into the baking dish. Chill 1 hour in refrigerator. Preheat oven to 350° and bake until firm, for about 1 hour.

Remove pudding from the oven and allow to cool on rack until just warm. Place the square of the pudding on a plate. Add a dollop of heavy whipped cream, dust with powdered sugar, and garnish with fresh mint sprigs.

Maine Blueberry Cake

1 cup sugar
½ cup shortening
2 unbeaten eggs
2 cups all-purpose flour
2½ teaspoons baking powder
½ teaspoon salt
½ cup milk
½ teaspoon vanilla
1 cup blueberries, fresh or frozen

Cream together the sugar and shortening; add the unbeaten eggs and mix well. In a medium bowl, sift together the flour, baking powder and salt and add to the egg mixture alternately with the milk. Stir in the vanilla. Flour the blueberries by shaking them in a bag with 1 tablespoon of flour. Gently fold the blueberries into the batter.

Pour batter into a greased square cake pan and bake at 350° for 30–45 minutes until toothpick inserted in center comes out clean.

As cake cools, sprinkle with cinnamon and sugar. May be served warm or cold, with ice cream.

Contributed by Ginny Gass

Exotic Fruit Bake

8 ounces fresh (or canned) pineapple
8 ounces fresh (or canned) mango
2 tablespoons dark rum
3 eggs, beaten
3½ tablespoons all-purpose flour
Pinch of salt
1¼ cups superfine sugar, plus extra for sprinkling
1¼ cups milk
1 vanilla bean
Vanilla ice cream

Peel the fresh pineapple and mango. Cut the flesh into ½ inch chunks. Put the prepared fruit in a bowl and sprinkle with rum. Set aside while making the batter. Break the eggs into a bowl and beat lightly together. Sift the flour and salt, and blend well with the beaten eggs. Whisk in the sugar until smooth. Heat the milk with the vanilla bean but do not bring to a boil. Remove mixture from heat and let stand for 5 minutes. Remove the vanilla bean and strain milk into the egg mixture, a little at a time, beating well until it is thoroughly blended. Beat in the rum from the soaked fruit.

Arrange the pineapple and mango in a shallow, greased ovenproof dish. Pour the batter mixture over the fruit and bake in a preheated oven at 400° for 25–30 minutes, until risen and set. Cool slightly and serve warm with sprinkled sugar and vanilla ice cream.

Chocolate Mousse Pie

CRUST

3 cups chocolate wafer crumbs
1½ cups unsalted butter, melted

Combine crumbs and butter and press on bottom and sides of 10 inch spring form pan. Refrigerate for 30 minutes or chill in freezer.

FILLING

1 pound semisweet chocolate
2 eggs
4 egg yolks
2 cups whipping cream
6 tablespoons powdered sugar
4 egg whites, room temperature

Soften chocolate in top of double boiler over simmering water. Let cool to luke warm temperature. Add whole eggs and mix well. Add yolks and mix until thoroughly blended. Whip cream with powdered sugar until soft peaks form. Beat egg whites until stiff but not dry. Stir a little of the cream and egg whites into chocolate mixture to lighten. Fold in remaining cream and egg whites until completely incorporated. Turn chocolate mixture into crust and chill overnight.

CHOCOLATE LEAVES

8 ounces semisweet chocolate, melted
1 tablespoon vegetable shortening
Camellia or other waxy leaves

Melt chocolate and shortening in top of double boiler. Using spoon, generously coat underside of leaves. Chill or freeze leaves until firm.

ASSEMBLY

2 cups heavy cream – whipped

Whip remaining 2 cups of cream until stiff. Loosen crust on all sides using sharp knife to remove crust from spring form pan. Spread all but ½ cup of cream over the top of mousse. Pipe remaining cream into rosette in center of pie.

Separate chocolate from leaves, starting at stem end of leaf. Arrange in overlapping pattern around rosettes.

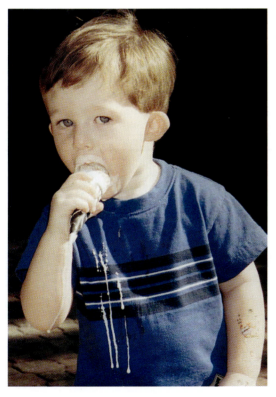

Grandson Austin enjoys an ice cream at the zoo.

Three Ginger Gingerbread

3 cups all-purpose flour
1 tablespoon ground cinnamon
2 teaspoons baking soda
1½ teaspoons ground cloves
1 teaspoon ground ginger
¾ teaspoons salt
1½ cups sugar
1 cup vegetable oil
1 cup light molasses (unsulfured)
½ cup water
2 large eggs
1 tablespoon fresh ginger, minced
½ cup crystallized ginger

Preheat oven to 350°. Butter and flour 10 inch spring form pan. Sift first 6 ingredients in a medium bowl. In a large bowl, combine sugar, oil, molasses, water, eggs and fresh ginger. Whisk to blend. Mix in crystallized ginger. Stir in dry ingredients and mix well. Pour batter into prepared pan.

Bake until center of cake comes out clean, about 1 hour. Cool cake in pan on rack for 1 hour. Wrap cake in foil and refrigerate. Bring to room temperature before serving.

Cheesecake

CRUST

1¾ cups of Graham cracker or/digestive biscuit crumbs
¼ cup chopped walnuts
½ teaspoon cinnamon
½ cup butter, melted

Mix all ingredients together. Press into bottom and sides of a 9 inch spring form pan.

FILLING

3 eggs
2 8-ounce packets cream cheese, softened
1 cup sugar
2 teaspoons vanilla extract
3 cups sour cream
1 small can pineapple, crushed (optional)

Combine eggs, cheese, sugar, vanilla and crushed pineapple. Beat on medium until smooth. Blend in sour cream. Pour into crust and bake at 375° for one hour. Chill overnight. Serve with whipped cream.

Date Nut Balls

8 ounces butter
2 8-ounce packets dates, chopped
1 box light brown sugar
1 cup coconut
1 cup nuts, chopped
3 cups Rice Krispies cereal
½ cup powdered sugar

Place butter, dates and brown sugar in saucepan and bring to rapid boil; cook for 6 minutes. Add coconut, nuts, and cereal. Cool.

Form into small balls. Put powdered sugar in zip lock bag and add balls a dozen at a time, coating with sugar. Shake off excess. Chill in refrigerator.

Contributed by Liz Hill

Granddaughter Caitlin is dressed up and ready for dessert!

Breakfast, Brunch and Breads

Breakfast Casserole

12 large eggs
3 cups milk
½ pound mild pork sausage
½ pound spicy pork sausage (or regular sausage with cayenne pepper added)
1 small onion, finely chopped
1 cup mushrooms, thinly sliced
2 cups cheddar cheese, shredded
6 slices white bread, crusts removed and cut into 1-inch pieces
2 tablespoons olive oil

Heat a little oil in pan and cook sausage meat. Drain. Cook onions and mushrooms until tender, 4–5 minutes.

Layer bread, sausage, onions, mushrooms and cheese in an ovenproof dish. Combine eggs and milk and mix well. Pour egg mixture over bread mixture. Refrigerate overnight.

Bake at 350° for 45 minutes.

Contributed by Nicki Aronson

Gruyère Soufflé

4 tablespoons butter
1½ cups Gruyère cheese, grated
3 tablespoons flour
1½ cups hot milk
4 extra large egg yolks
5 extra large egg whites, beaten very stiff
Salt and pepper

Preheat oven to 375°. Butter a 6 cup soufflé dish and sprinkle the sides and bottom with cheese.

Heat remaining butter in saucepan. When butter is hot, add flour and stir quickly. Cook for 1 minute. Pour in hot milk and mix well with whisk. Season with salt and pepper and cook for 8 minutes over low heat, stirring frequently.

Remove saucepan from heat and let cool slightly. Add egg yolks one at a time, whisking between additions until yolks are incorporated into batter. Transfer batter to a bowl; stir in remaining cheese. Gently fold beaten egg whites into batter, being careful not to over mix. Pour batter into soufflé dish. (Batter should be 1½ inches from top of dish.)

Bake for 35–40 minutes. Serve hot.

Onion Tart

1 cup sour cream
2 cups heavy cream
4 eggs
1 egg yolk
White pepper to taste
1 teaspoon salt
3 large onions, finely chopped
1 tablespoon olive oil
1 9 inch round x 2 inch high unbaked pie shell formed in a flan
2 slices thick cut bacon, chopped

Preheat oven to 350°. Heat oil, add onions and cook until just tender; set aside. Whisk together sour cream, heavy cream, eggs, egg yolk, salt and pepper. Stir in onion. Pour mixture into unbaked pie shell. Sprinkle bacon evenly on top.

Bake tart for 1 hour or until custard is lightly set (knife in center of tart should come out clean).

Cool for 30 minutes. Unmold and serve at room temperature.

Raspberry Nut Muffins

½ cup butter or margarine, softened
1 cup sugar
2 eggs
½ cup milk
2 cups all-purpose flour
2 teaspoons baking powder
½ teaspoon salt
1½ cups raspberries (frozen or fresh)
¼ cup chopped nuts (pecans preferred)
1 tablespoon sugar

Preheat oven to 425°. Grease muffin tins or use paper inserts. Cream butter and sugar; add one egg at a time; beat well. Combine dry ingredients. Alternately add milk and dry ingredients to butter, sugar, and eggs. Fold in raspberries carefully; add chopped nuts. Fill muffin tin. Sprinkle 1 tablespoon sugar on top of muffins. Bake for 25–30 minutes.

Stuffed French Toast with Apricot-Orange Sauce

8 ounces cream cheese, softened
1/4 cup walnuts, chopped
1 large loaf French bread
8 ounces apricot jam
1/2 cup orange juice
3 eggs
1/2 cup milk
1 teaspoon vanilla
1/4 teaspoon cinnamon
4–6 ounces butter, melted

Cut French bread loaf in half, lengthways. Mix nuts with cream cheese. Spread cheese mixture on one half of bread; spread 4 ounces jam on other half of bread. Sandwich together both halves of bread loaf and cut loaf into 2-inch slices.

Mix together milk, eggs, vanilla and cinnamon. Dip sandwiches in bowl with egg mixture. Let soak 15 minutes. Heat butter in pan and gently grill slices until golden brown.

Combine orange juice and apricot jam; heat gently. Drizzle warm apricot-orange sauce over top of sandwiches and serve immediately.

Cranberry-Orange Bread

3 medium oranges
1 beaten egg
2 tablespoons cooking oil
2 cups all-purpose flour
¾ cup granulated sugar
1½ teaspoons baking powder
1 teaspoon salt
½ teaspoon baking soda
1 cup fresh or frozen cranberries, coarsely chopped
½ cup walnuts, chopped
1 cup powdered sugar, sifted

Finely shred 1 orange peel; reserve peel. Squeeze juice from all oranges. Measure ¾ cup of juice; reserve remaining juice. In a mixing bowl combine ¾ cup orange juice, 1 teaspoon of shredded orange peel, egg and cooking oil. In another mixing bowl, stir together flour, granulated sugar, baking powder, salt and baking soda. Add orange juice mixture to dry ingredients, stir until moistened. Fold in chopped cranberries and walnuts.

Turn batter into one lightly greased 8 x 4 x 2 inch loaf pan or 3 (6 x 3 x 2) inch pans. Bake 50–60 minutes for large (30–40 for smaller) or till wooden pick inserted near center comes out clean. Cool bread 10 minutes in pan, then remove and cool thoroughly on wire rack.

For glaze, stir 1 tablespoon of juice into powdered sugar. Add more juice if needed for thinner consistency. Drizzle glaze over cooled loaves, and garnish with reserved orange peel.

Baked Apple Pancakes

In one bowl combine:
2 medium apples, (a sweeter apple is best) peeled and sliced very thin

Add:
⅓ cup of light brown sugar
1 teaspoon cinnamon
2 tablespoons butter or margarine, melted

In second bowl combine well:
½ cup flour
½ cup milk (2% is fine)
2 eggs mixed well
Pinch of salt

Preheat oven to 425°. Melt 2 extra tablespoons butter in a 9-inch glass pie plate; pour in flour and milk mixture. Place fruit mixture in center of pie plate. Bake 15 minutes. Sprinkle pancakes with powdered sugar and serve immediately.

Irish Scones

2 cups all purpose flour
2 ounces butter, chilled and cut into small pieces
¼ cup sugar
¼ cup raisins (optional)
½ teaspoon cream of tartar
1 teaspoon baking powder
¾ cup buttermilk
1 egg, lightly beaten

Sift flour, baking powder, and cream of tartar into large bowl. Add butter and rub in until mixture resembles fine breadcrumbs. Add sugar and raisins. Mix buttermilk and egg together – should measure 1 cup. Make a well in the center of the flour mixture and add half of buttermilk. Mix well and slowly add remaining buttermilk until mixture comes together to form soft dough. If mixture is too sticky, add more flour.

Turn onto well-floured board and gently knead together. Be careful not to over knead, as this will make scones heavy. Roll out dough to 1-inch thickness and cut into rounds with medium-sized cutter. (Makes 8–10 scones).

Place scones on lightly floured baking tray and bake for 12–15 minutes in a 425° oven.

NOTE: Scones are delicious served with whipped cream and strawberry jam.

Irish Soda Bread

2 tablespoons butter, softened
2½ cups all-purpose flour
2 tablespoons sugar
1 teaspoon baking soda
1 teaspoon baking powder
¼ cup raisins (optional)
¾ cup buttermilk

Cut butter into flour; add sugar, baking soda, baking powder, raisins, and salt. Stir until mixture resembles fine breadcrumbs. Add enough buttermilk to form soft dough. Turn dough onto well-floured board and knead gently until smooth.

Shape dough into 6 inch round; place on greased baking sheet and cut a deep "X" (about ¼ inch) through top of bread using a floured knife.

Bake bread at 375° for 35–40 minutes until golden brown. Remove from oven and serve warm with lots of butter.

Left to right: daughter Kathy and her husband Mike, Bob's brother Neil,
son Neil and his wife Jacki, Helen and David (Debby's folks).

MEASURING EQUIVALENTS

IMPERIAL	AMERICAN
1 teaspoon	1 teaspoon
1 tablespoon	1 tablespoon
1½ tablespoons	2 tablespoons
2 tablespoons	3 tablespoons
3 tablespoons	scant ¼ cup
4 tablespoons	5 tablespoons (½ cup)
5 tablespoons	6 tablespoons
5½ tablespoons	7 tablespoons
6 tablespoons (scant ¼ pint)	½ cup
¼ pint	⅔ cup
scant ½ pint	1 cup
½ pint (10 fluid oz.)	1¼ cups
¾ pint (15 fluid oz.)	scant 2 cups
generous ¾ pint (16 fluid oz.)	2 cups (1 pint)
1 pint (20 fluid oz.)	2½ cups

Flour – plain or self-raising:	Flour – all purpose:
½ ounce	2 tablespoons
1 ounce	¼ cup
4 ounces	1 cup

Cornflour:	Cornstarch:
1 ounce	¼ cup
generous 2 oz.	½ cup
4½ oz.	1 cup

IMPERIAL	AMERICAN
Sugar – castor granulated:	Sugar – granulated:
1 ounce	2 tablespoons
4 ounces	½ cup
7½ ounces	1 cup
Sifted icing sugar:	Sifted confectioners' sugar
1 ounce	¼ cup
4½ ounces	1 cup
Sugar – soft brown:	Brown sugar – light & dark
1 ounce	2 tablespoons (firmly packed)
4 ounces	½ cup (firmly packed)
8 ounces	1 cup (firmly packed)
Butter, margarine, cooking fat, lard, drippings:	Butter, margarine, shortening, lard, drippings:
1 ounce	2 tablespoons
8 ounces	1 cup
Grated cheese – Cheddar type, Parmesan:	Grated cheese – Cheddar type Parmesan:
1 ounce	¼ cup
4 ounces	1 cup
8 ounces	2 cups

US Standard Measuring Spoons

EQUIPMENT, TERMS & INGREDIENTS

BRITISH	AMERICAN	BRITISH	AMERICAN
EQUIPMENT AND TERMS		Cocoa powder	Unsweetened cocoa
		Cooking apple	Baking apple
Baked/unbaked	Baked/unbaked	Cooking chocolate	Unsweetened cook-
pastry case	pie shell		ing chocolate
Baking tin	Baking pan	Cornflour	Cornstarch
Base	Bottom	Courgettes	Small zucchini
Cocktail stick	Toothpick	Crystallised fruits	Candied fruits
Dough or mixture	Batter	Crystallised ginger	Candied ginger
Frying pan	Skillet	Demerara sugar	Light brown sugar
Greaseproof paper	Wax paper	Digestive biscuits	Graham crackers
Grill/Grilled	Broil/Broiled	Double cream	Whipping cream
Gut fish	Clean fish	Dried breadcrumbs	Dry breadcrumbs
Kitchen paper	Paper towels	Essence	Extract
Knock back dough	Punch down dough	Fine breadcrumbs	Fine dry breadcrumbs
Mixer/Liquidiser	Mixer/Blender	Icing	Frosting
Pudding basin	Oven proof bowl	Icing sugar	Confectioners' sugar
Whip/Whisk	Beat/Whip	Peeled shrimps	Shelled shrimp
		Plain chocolate	Semi-sweet chocolate
INGREDIENTS		Plain flour	All-purpose flour
		Raising agent	Leavening agent
Aubergin	Eggplant	Root ginger	Ginger root
Bacon rashers	Bacon slices	Scones	Biscuits
Bicarbonate of Soda	Baking soda	Self-raising flour	All-purpose flour sifted
Biscuits	Crackers		with baking powder
Cake mixture	Bake batter	Single cream	Coffee cream
Biscuit mixture	Cookie dough	Soft brown sugar	Light brown sugar
Cake mixture	Cake batter	Soured cream	Cultured sour cream
Chicken/Beef	Bouillon cube	Stem ginger	Preserved ginger
stock cube		Sultanas	Seedless white raisins
Chilli	Chili pepper		

INDEX OF RECIPES